KATE'S
SECRET
RIDDLE
BOOK

KATE'S SECRET RIDDLE BOOK

BY SID FLEISCHMAN
illustrated by Barbara Bottner

AN EASY-READ STORY BOOK

FRANKLIN WATTS | NEW YORK | LONDON | 1977

Library of Congress Cataloging in Publication Data

Fleischman, Albert Sidney.
    Kate's secret riddle book.

    (An Easy-read story book)
    SUMMARY: Kate's brother collects several rid-
dles while trying to find the question to the answer
of a riddle told them by a friend.
    [1. Riddles—Fiction] I. Bottner, Barbara. II. Title.
PZ7.F5992Kat   [E]   76-56160
ISBN 0-531-00377-9 lib. bdg.
ISBN 0-531-01334-0

FOR KATE EMILY

I hope you don't have a friend like
Wally. He lives across the street.

Wally is always doing mean tricks.
And then he flaps his arms like a
dumb chicken and laughs.

On Saturday he rang our doorbell.
"Let me in, Jimmy," he said.
"No," I said. "My sister is sick."

"I want to tell her a riddle. It will make her laugh."

I hadn't been able to make Kate laugh all week.

"Do you want to hear a riddle?"
Wally asked.

"No," Kate said.

"It's a funny riddle."

"Well, okay," Kate said.

"Ready? Here's the riddle. *Doggone!*"
I said, "That's not a riddle!"
"It's the answer to one. You've got
to think of the question. That's
the funny part!"

He flapped his arms like a chicken.
He laughed all the way out of the
house.

"I feel sick," Kate said.

"You're already sick," I said.

"I feel sicker. He'll never tell us
the riddle."

"Maybe someone else knows it.
I'll be back," I said.

I met the postman at the front door.
"Do you know any riddles, Mr. Hunt?"
Mr. Hunt scratched his head. "What
did the fly say when he fell into
melted butter?"
"Doggone," I answered.
"Nope." He said, " 'look! I'm a
butterfly.' "

At the store I asked Mrs. Mitchell,
"Do you know any riddles?"
"Let me think. If you put a clock in
a beehive, what time would it be?"
"I give up."
"Why, it would be hive o'clock," Mrs.
Mitchell smiled.

I helped Mr. Snow out with his bags.

"Do you know any riddles, sir?"

"Of course I do. If ducks say quack-quack when they walk, what do they say when they run?"

"Doggone?" I asked.

"They say 'Quick! Quick!' "

Maybe Wally had made up that
crazy answer.
But it gave me an idea.
I ran back to the store and bought
a small school pad. I'd write down
all the riddles before I forgot any.

Just about everyone I met had a
riddle to tell me.

what did the crow
say after eating
Mrs. Smith's
strawberrys?
            Thank you
            berry .much.

How did three sardines
walk across the road?

        Don't be silly.
Sardines can't walk.

What do you get if you
leave a ruler near a
spider?

a webbed foot.

What does a toad sit
on?

a toadstool.

The book was almost full when I saw
Miss Smith. "Oh, I know a riddle,"
she said. "What side of a house gets
the most rain?"
"I don't know, Miss Smith."
"The outside."

I wrote it down. Just then something happened across the street. Mr. Cross's dog got out of the yard and ran away. Mr. Cross gave an angry shout.

And I gave a whoop. I knew the
question to Wally's riddle!

I wrote it in the book. On the
cover I printed
KATE'S SECRET RIDDLE BOOK.
I ran home as fast as I could.

Before long Kate was laughing so
hard that Wally could hear her.
He came to the window. "What
are you laughing at?"

"Your riddle," Kate answered.

"*Doggone*. Wally, that's the funniest
riddle in the whole world."

"It is?" Wally said.

"I can't stop laughing," Kate said.

"Tell me the first part," begged
Wally.

"Oh, you know it."

Wally said, "No, I don't. I just made
up that doggone answer to tease you.
I don't know the question."

"You're just pretending," Kate
laughed. "Oh, it's so funny. But
don't worry. Jimmy and I promise to
keep it a secret."

"Come on and tell me," Wally said.

"You're looking kind of sick, Wally,"
Kate said.

"You'd better go home to bed.
Goodbye. I'm feeling so much
better."

She held up the book and read
the last riddle again.

5 What do you say
when your dog runs
away?

Dog- gone!

Good job

a

(Don't tell Wally.)

ABOUT THE AUTHOR

Sid Fleischman may be best known as the creator of the most "honest" man in the world – Josh McBroom. He has, however, also given young readers many other novels, in addition to his famous tall-tale series.

His numerous awards include the Lewis Carroll Award, and the Society of Children's Book Writers Award. He is an ex-newspaperman and an ex-magician. But once a magician always a magician, as he proves with his tricks in KATE'S SECRET RIDDLE BOOK.